# PURE

**By Latrica Saygo**

## Dedication

To all the young women that are facing things that you can't see the light in the midst of the hurt. It's only a season. Sometimes the truth is the only way to overcome. Face it, embrace it, and trust you first. It's a healing process. Its growth. Some of the best had to go through it.

## Table of contents

**1 – 1 part water 1 part dirt**

**2-The Mudd that made me**

**3-How deep is your Mudd**

**4- Incalculable Mudd**

**5-I'm drowning in Mudd**

**6- Is this mudd or quicksand**

## Introduction

**What if I told you that life isn't really hard and that there is a cheat code to it. Would you believe me? What if I told you that I could relate to many of your life experiences and got through them before the age of 25. How many times have you talked or prayed yourself out of something only to be exactly back where you started to begin praying your way out of it because you were not knowledgeable of the situation at hand. Don't stop reading; it only gets deeper from here on out.**

## CHAPTER1
## 1 PART WATER, 1 PART DIRT

My life started out great as a child who seemed to have everything a child could want. I had parents that were married and together. A mother who always puts her children and husband ahead of anything. A father that worked to provide and protect his family by any means necessary. I had siblings that I could go to for anything. I could say I had a nice bond with a huge extended family on both sides of the family. Both sets of grandparents were alive, and I got to see them grow old and pass on. Oh, and the typical dysfunctional family ish, y'all know what I'm talking about.

Though I wasn't your typical child, most people would consider this crazy, but I remember climbing out of my crib night after night and my parents waking up stunned at how I did it, and I had to be about 4 months. I clearly remember hanging from my dad's jerry curl at about 6 months or so. I remember my sisters playing and running. I hated it so much that I couldn't get up and run or play like them, and I made up my mind right there that I was going to run before I walked, and that's exactly what I did, true story. At 2 years old, I remember my mom making dinner for my siblings and me one evening, and she was doing one of my sisters' hair or something. She told me that she would make my plate as soon as she was finished. I definitely did not want to wait, apparently because I reached into the pot of water and burned my whole left side. Yup, you guessed it, the hospital burn unit the whole nine. Guess what; I didn't cry. They thought my mother was the patient because she was doing all the crying. 3 years later, we moved to Beloit, Wisconsin, and we were watching television; my dad told us that we could have ice cream after the game went off; he must have gone to sleep or something. I was very disappointed and decided to do something terrible. I guess I decided to bite an electrical cord to wake him up, and that's exactly what I did. I actually bit a cord that had an electrical current running through it. My hair stood up, my teeth were black, and my eyebrows were gone!! I did not cry. You know what I said, IT DIDN'T HURT. This event is always brought up in family meetups. A couple of months later, I'm stuck in a tree by the hood of my coat, and I'm not talking of the bottom of the tree so someone can just pull me down; nope, I was at the top of the tree. Everyone went into the house, and my parents were asking where I was, and I was outside, hanging around, literally just enjoying the view. My brother saving me from becoming a part of a bird's nest was the best. I was something else. Prone to a mishap at a young age and handle it with a class, so to speak.

I can remember being in kindergarten and being one of the smartest students in the class. Of course, being a very student came with perks. Helping the teacher with things while other students had to do homework or being able to take things to other classrooms without the assistance of a faculty member. Staying after school or coming to school early to set up things for the next day of school. I loved my teacher, her name is

Mrs. Hernandez. I remember being the fastest runner in school at my age and grade. When it came to field day I could hardly wait. I knew I would get all the ribbons for first place. I loved racing anyone that was up for a challenge. I met friends in kindergarten that I am still in contact with today, even though I am 37 years old. That was the solid foundation of years to come. I went through elementary school with being on honor roll and a couple of favorite teachers that I

thank for being there when a student needed them most. My Six grade teacher was the most memorable of all. Mr. Hillmer touched so many students' lives in so many ways; it’s immeasurable. My sixth-grade year of elementary school prepared me for middle school, and I'm not talking grade-wise; I mean mentally. I was able to go into 7th grade with confidence and was a very smart student. My childhood was something I can reflect on and say I knew exactly why I did some of the things I did, and I knew at a young age why I did them. I remember having to go to church every single Sunday. My mom made me, and all my sisters and my aunties made my cousins go to church every Sunday as well.

My grandfather was a pastor, so every Sunday like clockwork, we packed a blue station wagon he had and drove to Chicago, Illinois, every Sunday. My faith in God has always been there from what I can remember. The love for God had been instilled from a very young age, and through those instilled values, I was able to rely on him. My faith in God was huge. My relationship grew the most upon reaching 7th grade. In7th grade, I was more of the honor roll student and sports typical kid childhood. The summer leading to 8th grade was the summer that would shape the woman I am today.

## CHAPTER 2

### THE MUDD THAT MADE ME...,

### *My life took a whole left turn .....*

Summer of 97, I met a friend. We had been living on the same street since I was in 3rd grade, so when new people moved into the area, we knew who they were. I became great friends with one of the girls that moved to the block. I remember seeing the most beautiful black girl I had ever met. She was dark-complexioned and had the most beautiful hair. It was really long, and she had ponytails that hung past her shoulders. She was outside playing, and my cousin and I were walking and playing, and I remember her saying, "Hey, y'all want to play?" And the rest was history. I didn't know it then, but she would become my right-hand man for years to come. A few months passed, and she told me her brother was asking about me or something of that nature. Now, I'm nervous because I've never had a boy even look my way. If they did, I beat them up. This was different. As months passed, we grew closer to one another. The kid love taps, they would say. Acting like we didn't like each other and kissing on the side of the house type of relationship. I should've known it was toxic from the start. Things started to happen. This was the first time that a boy gave me that kind of attention. When I tell you I fell hard, I mean that in the most deteriorating way.

By the time school started back up in the fall, I had a whole relationship going on that I didn't quite understand myself. Everything happened so fast. I went to homecoming with the guy and thought maybe this could work right. WRONG ..... 3 months later, my mom and dad called me in the house and said, if you are having sex, tell us because you are going to the doctor to get some birth control. I had just turned 14. I responded, "Well, you better give me something." My sister, who's 2years older than me, was being taken to the doctor because my parents believed she was pregnant. We were two doors away from each other in the doctor's office. My older sister was going from one room to the next. The results? BOTH PREGNANT!! Hell was about to break loose. We both are crying, and both scared at the same time. We walk into the house, and she tells them the results. My mother was in tears and told us how we would work to raise these babies. My father, well, let's just say he made plenty of snow angels that night while crying hysterically. This was not a pretty scene. Trust me; you wouldn't have wanted to be there. So now I'm a baby having a baby. I'm not ready, well, at least for what's about to happen to me. At that age, I was about to be a teen mom and be going to 8th grade. All my friends were still doing kid things, and I had to fuck up. I felt I was about to lose my friends due to the fact that I was only 14 and pregnant. I'm sure their parents didn't want their daughters around me, at least in my head. After finding out about the news, I was just consumed with all kinds of thoughts of what a real fuck up I was. I couldn't stop thinking of all the things that everyone would say about me. I had a conversation with my mom one day about this, and she told me, "People are going to talk about you if you are doing bad, and they will talk about you if you're doing good, so let them talk." At that moment, I realized one thing, this is my life, and how I choose to live it is up to me. I began to prepare my mind for the child that I was bringing into this world. I often caught myself daydreaming about what this little human would become. What would his/her character be like?

I believed that though it happened at such a young age, I would be able to mentally prepare, if not, nothing else.

## CHAPTER 3
## How deep is your mudd

I'm 14 in the 8th grade and pregnant. What kind of horror story am I living in? I've gone from straight A's to pregnant and expelled from middle school. Yes, I said expelled. I literally am dealing with morning sickness and 3 months pregnant when some girl decided this was a great time to slam a locker door on my pregnant belly, and when I walked away, she wrapped her book bag purse around her hand and hit me in the head and face with it. Let's just say when I came to, I had 3-4 officers holding me down, and my mom had to come pick me up. I blacked completely out, and the girl, well, she will never hit another pregnant woman again. So now I must go to court and to an alternative school to finish out my last year of middle school until I

am allowed back into the regular school system. Now, let me warn you, the shit is about to get real deep. I'm gonna take you through my 14-year-old pregnant life. I'm 14. I'm being introduced to things a 14-year-old girl should not be exposed to at this age, at least. My son's dad is completely out of control with cheating and having babies. We fight like forty going north, I'm still in a relationship with him. He's still doing whatever his heart desires—at the same time, dangling me by a string. My feelings were hurt, I was completely embarrassed, I had low self-esteem because I was constantly being told I was ugly, and nobody wanted me. He has made a complete fool of me. I'm acting out in a number of ways that I could never even imagine. Times where I would just hide because I looked like a damn fool. When I tell you I was embarrassed and humiliated, that's an understatement. This boy is literally having whole situationships with a number of girls and still making it his business to control me. I'm pregnant and in a relationship with someone that's in a relationship with everyone but me. I was under so much stress; I didn't even know how I was going about my day because it was consumed with thoughts of what he was doing to me. He was so bold; he got one of them tattooed on his arm. Now when you are in lust because that wasn't love, however, I was sure I did love him. You watch and study everything that person does. We were in his mother's living room, and he forgot he got the tattoo. I tried to scratch the tattoo off his arm. Every single time he did something, it was like he was trying to outdo the last thing he did. He bought a ring and showed me like he was giving it to me and then gave it to the other girl. He later bought me a ring, and I ended up throwing it across St. Pat's Park. I'm seeing him get out of cars with the girl and her entire family like, what the fuck was I supposed to do? The series of events happened while I was pregnant. My life is completely a mess. When I confronted him about things, I've seen with my own two eyes and caught him, he wanted to fight, or use reverse psychology. So now I'm introduced to being hit by someone you love. I'm not saying I didn't hit him before he hit me from time to time, but it was all out of anger and embarrassment. I know no excuses. Most of the time, it was him being caught that angered him, and he'd want to beat me up. I'm getting bruises, black eyes, busted lips, stomping and all, and I'm taking it because I felt he would eventually change. I recall being accused of cheating with guys I hadn't even met before. I remember always buying things for him, and never will I really get to see him in it. He would get gifts and leave. Yes, I was a complete fool. One weekend during my pregnancy, my mom, sisters, and I planned a trip to Milwaukee, WI. It was a lady's link up with the rest of my family that lived there. He called me all kinds of names and made me feel so bad because I wanted to be with my family. I remember that I held back my tears on that whole drive there so no one would know how I really felt. That day I got to be with my family and not worry about anything back home. I remember coming back, and it was more of the verbal abuse and him telling me how much of a hoe I was and how he was about to go be with another girl. I cried so much; I felt like I had nothing left in my tear ducts. One day, a girl dropped him off at home, and I remember being so mad and hurt. I found the biggest stick I could find and chased him around the neighborhood with it, full speed; I was 9 months pregnant. Still, today, his brother brings that up. I know women are supposed to be happy and feel loved, and enjoy pregnancy, but how could I? I was literally living what love got to do with life. This entire time I was living with my parents, I was sneaking him in and out of windows. I turned into something that I never thought I'd become. 'How is this boy controlling me, and I don't even live with him?' I thought often. I was stealing my parents' cars and all just to see this boy. Have you ever made fun of someone, and they have this embarrassing look on their face? Well, I had that face all the time. I'd walk into stores, and people that knew us both would say, "You got pregnant by him; man, you don't deserve that; you're a good person and smart, leave him alone." I'd fan it off cause the truth was I knew I wasn't a bad person; I just didn't know how to live in my truth. The most mind-boggling thing was it wasn't like I didn't have a dad to show me love or a mother who didn't love me. They are great parents, and we never went out without them. I just fell hard, and I mean that in the most despicable way. I fell to the equivalent of someone being hooked on drugs. It was like I had to have him no matter how bad he treated me. I wrote, talked, and even tried to self-medicate, but nothing worked. I was stuck. The things that I endured just made me feel even uglier and shameful. I knew things that till this day he doesn't know I know. A woman's intuition is a muthaf**ka; I promise you that. I'll say that my intuition about him led me to every girl he ever cheated on me with and to him while he was cheating, TRUE STORY!! I remember my mom took me over to one of her friends' houses, and as soon as I entered her home, she began to pray for me. She then put her hands on my stomach and then began to pray for my unborn baby. She prayed, and she prayed. I remember being in a place where I just didn't want to live. I was so embarrassed. Day after day, more and more of my heart and mind were disassembling. All I remember saying to myself was, let me get through the pregnancy and have my son.

## CHAPTER 4

### INCALCULABLE MUDD

On August 9th, 1998, a king was born. James Allyn Robinson III. I became a mom at 14, and it was the first time I knew real love. My son was everything to me. I remember while in labor his dad was mad because I went into labor on his girl's bday. I couldn't predict that this would happen, but it did. After giving birth to my son, his dad seemed to be happy. I thought that maybe this would change him, maybe he would finally act right. Now I'm starting high school with a two-week-old baby. The first two weeks, I was doing what I was supposed to do, going to school, coming home with my baby, and doing homework. As my days became harder, there were rumors or truths that I didn't want to believe about him. I was dealing with postpartum depression, and I found out he was messing around with the girl with whom I go to school with. As if I wasn't already embarrassed enough. By this time, I was just angry and ready to tear anything and anyone up that had anything to say to me at all. I hated myself. I hated people altogether. I had people who really cared about me from his family and, of course, my own. They all just wanted me to leave him alone. So now I have enemies that I didn't even create. They were friends of females he was messing with. I was not the least bit worried about any of them because I was definitely about that action and TTG! (Trained to go). I started to slip badly. I mean, I couldn't function at all. It was like I was in a walking coma. I couldn't think of anything but what I was going through. I saw nothing but a straight path to him. The only other thing that I cared about was my son. I ate, slept, shit that boy. My son was growing, and I was always a mother to him regardless of what I was going through. I remember my son's nerves being so shot from the yelling and screaming that was going on that when I knew it was about to go down, I'd drop him off at my parents' house. The fights got worse; the cheating happened more often; the bitches got bolder. I should have listened earlier on. I remember being in class, and there was this girl talking about my son, and I literally waited for her at her locker to beat her up. I was just fucked up. I remember getting out of class to get water, and suddenly I felt something wasn't right. I felt very sad and on the verge of tears; my stomach was hurting. It was him. I walked out of the school and caught him at his house with the girl. We got into a fight. I remember just doing whatever I could to tear her apart. I was so angry that I bit her face while she was on the ground, and it was very ugly afterwards. I was out of control. I was in a rage and war with myself because I didn't know what to do or how to react anymore. It was so much. I've broken windows and fought this girl through a wall before. The things I've encountered at this age were ridiculous. A freshman in high school, how in the hell do you have a complete war with anyone that talks to you. One day I caught him, and he punched and stomped my face so hard I lost sight for an hour, and the next day I went to school and had to face him picking her up from school in my face. People looked at me and just covered their mouths. I was so gone, I didn't even care. He looked me dead in my face and waited for her to come out of the school. I still let him come and do whatever his heart desired. I was sick, slow, or both. I felt that no matter what, he would always come back. I just didn't know then that it was because I allowed him to. My parents and family were always there to tell me it was going to be ok and at the same time how stupid I was.

## CHAPTER 5

### I'M DROWNING IN MUDD

I remember my last day at that high school. I was in an algebra class, but I was not getting the information being taught. I asked the teacher if she could explain it in a different way to me; she told me no. I then remember getting up from my desk and walking out of the school one last time. At that point, I knew I had to do something if I wasn't going to go back to school. I caught the bus to the YMCA and filled out an application. I had to make a choice to work and take care of my son or go to school and fail because that's exactly what was happening. I chose to work, but that wasn't my parents' wishes; those were my own. Shit just got worse. I remember playing mokenstef repeatedly because my dumb ass believed he was mine. I always asked what I did to deserve this, and he always told me he loved me and that I was the best. Yea the best at being completely a damn fool. You would think, if I was the best, why was he doing this? I remember him writing me letters and drawing me pictures I kept for as long as I remember. That shit didn't matter, though, because he was doing the same exact thing for others. Him getting girl after girl pregnant. So now I have to deal with all that and continue getting hit and verbally abused. Walking around just dumb and numb. When I tell you that his one-up game was strong, man, listen, he was hitting family members and telling me OK. I remember him hiding me at his grandmother's house until she left for work. In my head I'm thinking why the hell I got to hide? I think he used to tell her I would tear shit up on purpose or something. When in reality, he created the anger that made me tear shit up. I'm 15, going on 16, working for the YMCA aftercare program. A high school dropout and being abused. Now I was never a lay down and do nothing type of person, but no matter what, I thought I was one thing for certain, I was being abused. I felt that the money I was making there was ok for a 16-year-old old but not good enough for a 16-year-old with a baby. I wanted more, and my mindset when it came to my son was, I got to get out of this I got to make some real money to care for him. I managed to enroll in an alternative school that allowed me to bring my son to school with me, so I didn't have to worry about a babysitter, so I did that for a couple of years or less then I found out his other baby mother went there. I might play a lot of games unconsciously when it comes to his dad and his bullshit, but not when it comes to my son. So, I had to get up outta there and can't really remember the time frame. However, I do remember the walking coma I was in because I could not grasp shitttt. It had to be 3 years or so. In that time, I took two more GED tests than I can remember and still could not manage to pass because I was not focused and could not retain anything with the stress and traumatization that I faced. I did, however, manage to obtain my CNA license and get a job.

That was the best thing I did, and I don't know how. When I graduated, he wasn't there to congratulate me at all. I had never been with anyone my entire life but him, and I was convinced that I was just stuck. I felt he was ashamed of me. I felt he was embarrassed to be with me or something. What was wrong with me? Why did God pick me for this to happen? I got my first apartment, and I was so proud of myself. Yup, you guessed it, he moved in. Now I have him living in my house and thinking he is going to do better ..NEGATIVE...... My family called me at work saying, "I saw him in your car with some girl. I saw some girl driving your car. I saw him picking some girl up from school in your car. I had girls showing up to my house while I was at work, girls in my car that he was driving around, and girls in my bed leaving their Jewelry in my house. I was so dumb that this boy got another girl pregnant; this dude would bring the baby to me to babysit while he went to find another girl to cheat with in my car. When I knew that he would be on one because I caught him, I would call my parents to come get my son so he would not be around the abuse. One specific day, I was at home alone. He left with my car. 2 carloads, full of girls pulled up; the girls beat on my windows and then proceeded to beat on my door and then left. I called him and asked him who he had been with and who he showed where I stayed. Of course, he denied everything like he didn't know what was going on. Smh, I recall him not even coming back home that night then, showing up with bloody boxers on and trying to convince me it was something else. I got to the point that I was just sick and tired but obviously not sick enough. Things got worse days and weeks and hell even months. He didn't come home, and I stayed home because he lived there with me as far as I knew. He would call or come home when I wasn't there to take his clothes or leave, just enough to let me know he was there and to make me hurt. I eventually moved out of that place and into another apartment. More and more of the same bullshit. I was working in New Milford at this packing company. I was really good friends with this lady. One night, she asked if I needed a ride home from work because sometimes, I caught rides when he was late to get me. This particular time, he just didn't show up. I walked 2 hours and 25 minutes to my home in the cold and snow. I was completely livid. He did not show up at the house for another 12 hrs., and when he did, I confronted him, and my son was there this time. He knocked me unconscious in front of my son and left. Imagine being unconscious, and your 6-year-old son is right there crying, and when you wake up, he tells you I thought you were dead. You think that would be enough, right? Wrong! This shit had to get better. That's what I thought. Another year of the same old shit. I

moved around the corner from my parents' house. The fact that I was so close, you'd think things would get better, lol. Nope, they didn't; him taking my car and not coming back. Me having to hide out in my own home so my parents wouldn't know he took my car for days. I'd have to find rides to go find my car parked down the street or around the corner from where he was at the other girl's house. I had no idea which house they lived in, so I couldn't just walk up to the door and ask for my keys. I just knew that every time someone told me something they saw, the majority came from a particular street. Until one day, I took off work to find out. I waited in the parking lot of the apartment complex and watched. He had no idea that I was watching. Out, he came, and boom, there was the info I needed. I told myself the next time he does this, I'm walking into the building. There shouldn't have ever been a damn first time. The girl was not clueless about what was going on. She knew about him and me because it was the same girl that was in my house, car, and the baby I watched was hers. It was a game to them but not to me. I think at that time; I was trying to see what made him want to be with her. He would tell me things about her, and I would say, if that's the case, why are you cheating on me with her. It was always his baby. Well, wtf about my baby? I let him build his relationship with our son. I never let my feelings get in that way, but he did. He just wouldn't or couldn't be there, and that was pure self-shit. He delivered blow after blow day after day. He cut hair, so sometimes he'd be there cutting some of his guy's hair, and sometimes I had to cut my son's hair. It was like a mask on, a mask off. Every single person in our town knew about us, but somehow, none of the girls gave a damn. This may have been the only house that he didn't pull a girl over, as far as I know. This mud was definitely knee-deep. The things I endured I thought I would never come out of.

## CHAPTER 6

## IS THIS MUDD OR QUICKSAND

In the summer of 2005, I was at a friend's house, and we were talking about relationships and all goals as usual. She says, "I'm taking a pregnancy test; you got to take one with me." I'm like,

"Why, I'm not pregnant." She said, "Please, just take one with me."

I obliged, and yup, guess what, I was pregnant. A complete shock because nothing was different; nothing changed with my body or anything. Everything was on schedule as it has been every month. I'm thinking like God, but I embraced it. So, I went to the doctor. Getting care is essential early, so I did what any normal pregnant woman does. I waited for him to come to my house, and I told him I was pregnant. He told me, "No, you're not." I showed him and watched him. I could tell he was becoming frustrated or something. He was saying something to me, and I remember saying it was a surprise to me too. We went back and forth, and then he got up and punched me as hard as he could in my stomach and kicked me. All I could do was cry. Nothing happened that day, but I went to the emergency room two days later because I was bleeding, and they confirmed that I had a miscarriage. That day, God showed me that this boy did not give one damn about the baby that was growing inside me nor about me. After that, I prayed and prayed about getting out of this situation-ship. I felt that I was starting to get closer to leaving, and there were times when God tested that notion. I knew I wasn't ready because as much as I was going through it, it was like I needed to endure this so I would never go through this again. Later, there was an episode where it was the 4th of July, and his other baby momma and her friends pulled up at my mom's house to fight because they saw my car parked there. My car!! Just know all hell broke loose, and it was a brawl. My family didn't play those kind of games. After the fight, he did not care one bit what happened to me or anything. I left him in 2006. I left, and when I did, I knew I was done. The things I mentioned are some of the things that transpired. I'd need a book collection to tell the story in deeper detail. I remember the day he had a court case, and I was there, and so was another girl. I asked to see the court papers that were given, and he gave them to her, but it wasn't that action that made me walk out and know it was over. It was how he looked at her for me. I immediately felt a weight being lifted off my shoulders, so I knew it was over. The final straw was leaving my son in the cold after school without even checking to see if he got in. My baby walked home by himself. I was so livid. At the fact that my child is having to see and hear from other kids that his dad doesn't love him. My child sees his dad being a father to his other kids but not him with his own eyes. So, I saw those things, and I couldn't allow him to keep hurting my son. So, I ended it, and I guess you can say that he then acted like my son didn't exist. We weren't mad at all. When my son had questions, I gave him the truth. I still don't know why his dad made their relationship the way he did. I never told him he couldn't be a part of his son's life. He chose that on his own, and I wasn't about to remind

you that you had a son over here. That wasn't who I was, or I will ever be. My relationship with my son is great. That's theirs, so I stay out of it. Quicksand is fast but not fast enough. I got up outta there just in time.

Acknowledgements

To my son . Thank you for coming into my life at such a tender age. You inspired me to do better. You were my why. Every day I reflect back on who I once was and thank GOD for you twice because it was you that I saw the light through. I will love you forever.

About the Author

Latrica Saygo is a wife and mother of three children. She was a teen mom and high school dropout, who later went on to pursue her GED and college degree and obtained her Associates degree in Business Administration from Colorado Technical University. She has a passion for mentoring youth of all ages. Her goals are to be an inspiration to all young women that face the same adversity and life struggles she faced at a young age and to be a resource to those that need help.

Also by Latrica Saygo

After The Mudd  June 2022

Made in the USA
Columbia, SC
31 January 2022